Aim high & be A star
#Proud American

2018

To ALL the Heroes that have made this country the greatest!

"And let us never forget that in honoring our flag, we honor the American men and women who have courageously fought and died for it over the last 200 years, patriots who set an ideal above any consideration of self. Our flag flies free today because of their sacrifice." ~ Ronald Reagan

10% of proceeds will go to Veterans charities.

Follow on:
www.OneFlagOneAmerica.com
facebook: OneFlagOneAmerica
instagram: OneFlagOneAmerica

Special Dedication: To my Grandfather, my Hero; George William Hirstius, Sr.
A Navy Veteran of World War II - December 3, 1921-December 11, 1997

Summary: This book explains what the American flag stands for in a fun way for children to learn. Included is a flag poem.

First Edition
ISBN-13: 978-0-9969410-4-4
ISBN-10: 0-9969410-4-5

Illustrations digitally done by: Michelle Hirstius

Fleur de Dat, LLC
P.O. Box 930
Mandeville, LA 70470-0930

www.fleurdedat.com

One Flag, One America
(the story of the American Star)

by: Michelle Hirstius

"Hi there, little star.
What are you doing here?"

"I'm waiting to be picked...
I'm a little star,
just a little star.
I wish and I pray,
that I'm a star on our
Nation's flag someday!"

"Why do you want to be on a flag?"

"Oh not just any flag, but the United States of America flag! It stands for liberty and freedom. I would shine brightly with 49 other stars. In the beginning there were only 13 stars but as America grew more were added. Today we have 50, one star for each state. Can you name ALL 50 states and show where they are on our country's map?"

AL-Alabama	IN-Indiana
AK-Alaska	IA-Iowa
AZ-Arizona	KS-Kansas
AR-Arkansas	KY-Kentucky
CA-California	LA-Louisiana
CO-Colorado	ME-Maine
CT-Connecticut	MD-Maryland
DE-Delaware	MA-Massachusetts
FL-Florida	MI-Michigan
GA-Georgia	MN-Minnesota
HI-Hawaii	MS-Mississippi
ID-Idaho	MO-Missouri
IL-Illinois	

MT-Montana	RI-Rhode Island
NE-Nebraska	SC-South Carolina
NV-Nevada	SD-South Dakota
NH-New Hampshire	TN-Tennessee
NJ-New Jersey	TX-Texas
NM-New Mexico	UT-Utah
NY-New York	VT-Vermont
NC-North Carolina	VA-Virginia
ND-North Dakota	WA-Washington
OH-Ohio	WV-West Virginia
OK-Oklahoma	WI-Wisconsin
OR-Oregon	WY-Wyoming
PA-Pennsylvania	

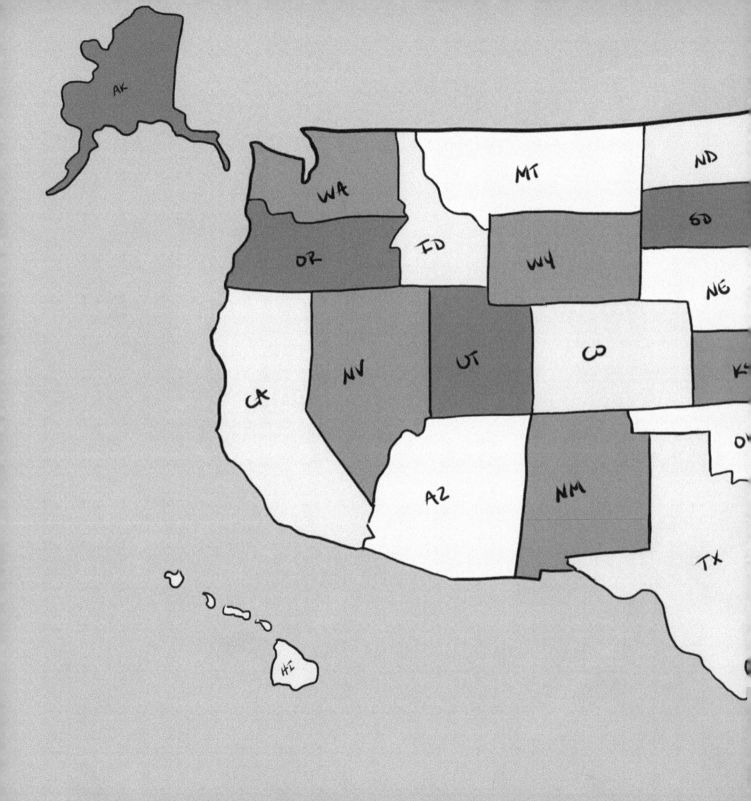

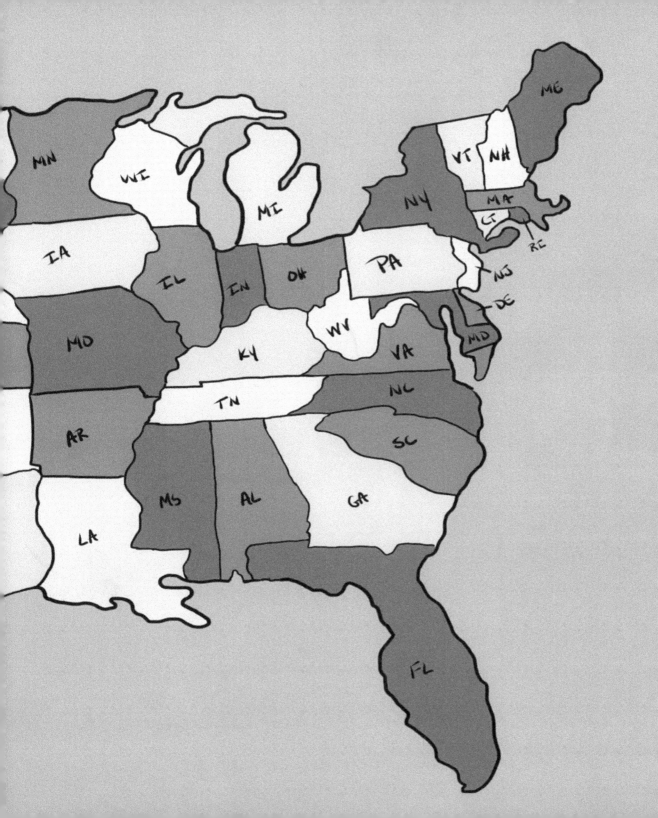

"The stars sound important, but what about the stripes?"

"They are too, there are 13 stripes. Each stripe is for a colony that became free from British rule. This happened on July 4th, 1776 after the Declaration of Independence was signed.

Can you name all 13 colonies that became states in 1788 and find them on the map?"

NH- New Hampshire
MA- Massachusetts
RI- Rhode Island
CT- Connecticut
NY- New York
NJ- New Jersey
PA- Pennsylvania
DE- Delaware
MD- Maryland
VA- Virginia
NC- North Carolina
SC- South Carolina
GA- Georgia

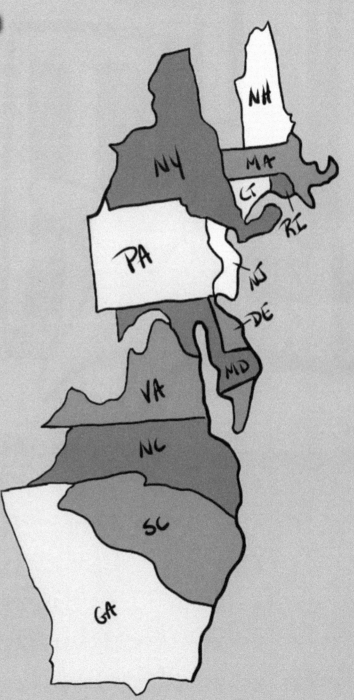

"I'm a little star,
just a little star.
I wish and I pray,
that I'm a star on our
Nation's flag someday!"

"Why are the colors of the flag red, white and blue?"

"These are the colors that America has stood for so long.

Red for hardiness and valor.
White for purity and innocence.
Blue for vigilance,
perseverance and justice.

All things that make our country great and strong."

"I'm a little star,
just a little star.
I wish and I pray,
that I'm a star on our
Nation's flag someday!"

"Wow!
The United States
of America's flag is
really special. How can
I show how proud
I am of the flag
and our country?"

"You can say the Pledge of Allegiance
and sing the National Anthem.
Be sure to stand tall
with your hand over your heart
and face the American flag."

The Pledge of Allegiance

"I pledge allegiance to the Flag
of the United States of America,
and to the Republic for which it stands,
one Nation under God,
indivisible, with liberty
and justice for all."

The National Anthem

"Oh, say, can you see, by the dawn's early light.
What so proudly we hailed at the twilight's last gleaming.
Whose broad stripes and bright stars, thro' the perilous fight'
O'er the ramparts we watched, were so gallantly streaming.
And the rockets red glare, the bombs bursting in air,
gave proof through the night that our flag was still there.
Oh, say, does that star-spangled banner yet wave,
O'er the land of the free and the home of the brave."

"So see why I stay and wait...
I'm a little star,
just a little star.
I wish and I pray,
that I'm a star on our
Nation's flag someday!"

"Here comes someone, little star!"

"I'm a little star,
but now not any star.
I wished, I prayed
and did not sway,
I'm a star on our
Nation's flag today!"

An American Star

Twinkle, twinkle little star,

I look up and there you are.

Up above on a pole so high,

with other stars and stripes you fly.

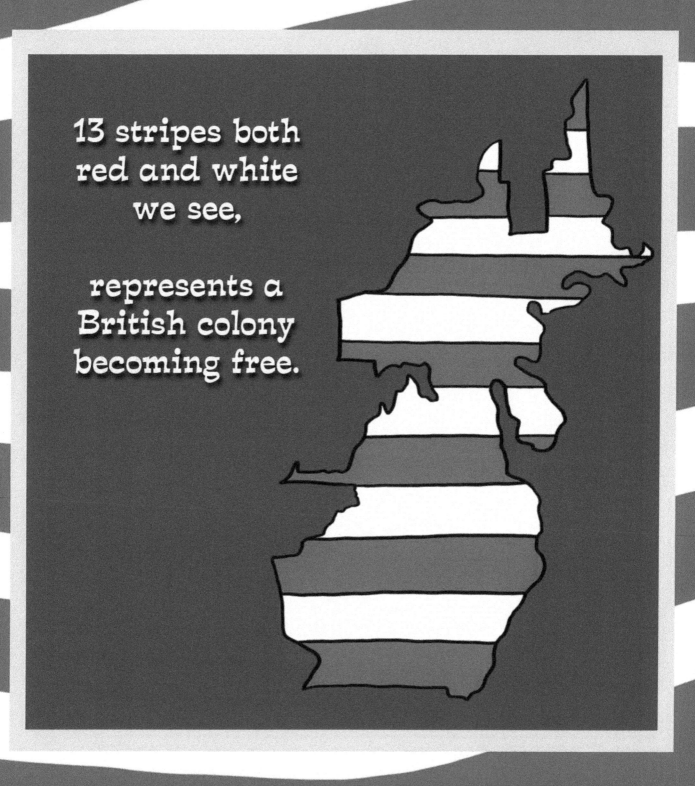

13 stripes both
red and white
we see,

represents a
British colony
becoming free.

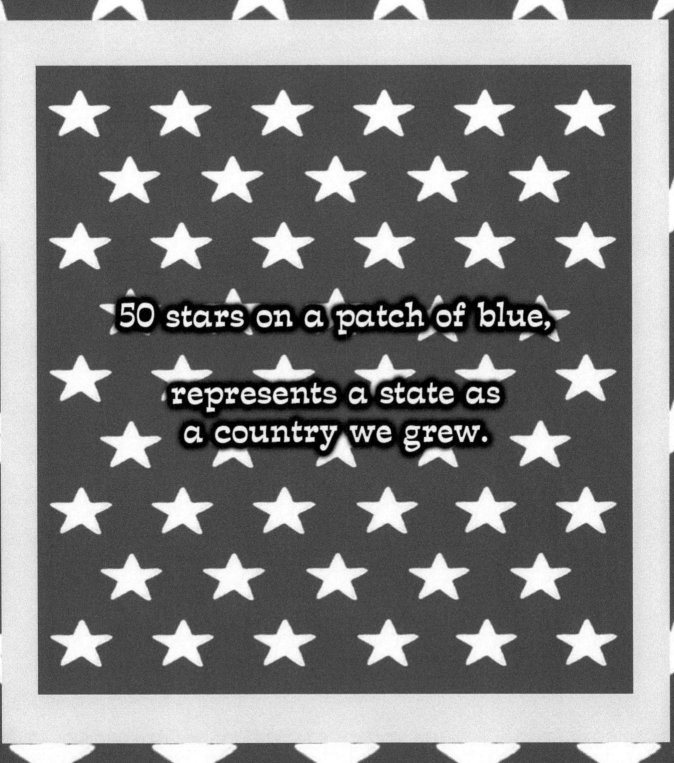

50 stars on a patch of blue,

represents a state as
a country we grew.

In front of you I stand tall,
I sing proudly and loud for all.

My hand over my heart,

you set our nation apart.

Representing a nation
together are we,

THANKS to our
heroes we are free.

At night we shine on you a light,

so that even in darkness
you are a hopeful sight.

One nation under God we stand,

Old Glory flies beautiful and grande.

Twinkle, twinkle little star,

there on our Nation's flag you are.

CPSIA information can be obtained
at www.ICGtesting.com
Printed in the USA
LVHW01*0320270218
567981LV00002BA/6/P